Copyright

© 2025 by Edward Shammas

All rights reserved. No part of this publication may be reproduced, distributed, or transmitted in any form or by any means, including photocopying, recording, or other electronic or mechanical methods, without the prior written permission of the publisher, except in the case of brief quotations embodied in critical reviews and certain other noncommercial uses permitted by copyright law.

Canadian Intellectual Property Office
Registration Number: 1229027, Registered on 13 DEC 2024
ISBN:979-8-9865339-2-6

Written by: Edward Shammas
Website: https://edwardshammas.com/
Email: eabshammas@gmail.com

Illustrations/Book layout : Mayssa Kennouche
Website: https://mayssakennouche.com/

For permissions, contact:
Edward Shammas

Arab Role Models: Dream, Lead, Inspire!

Edward Shammas

With art by Mayssa Kennouche

There are many special people from the arab world who have done amazing things!

They have talents in areas like science, arts, math, sports and more.

They show us that with hard work and dreams, we can do anything.

Let's meet some of them!

Maryam Maher
مريم ماهر

BAHRAIN

> "I got into gaming at a very young age. I started playing video games with my cousins, which is when my first obsession with gaming started."
> (Arora, 2020)

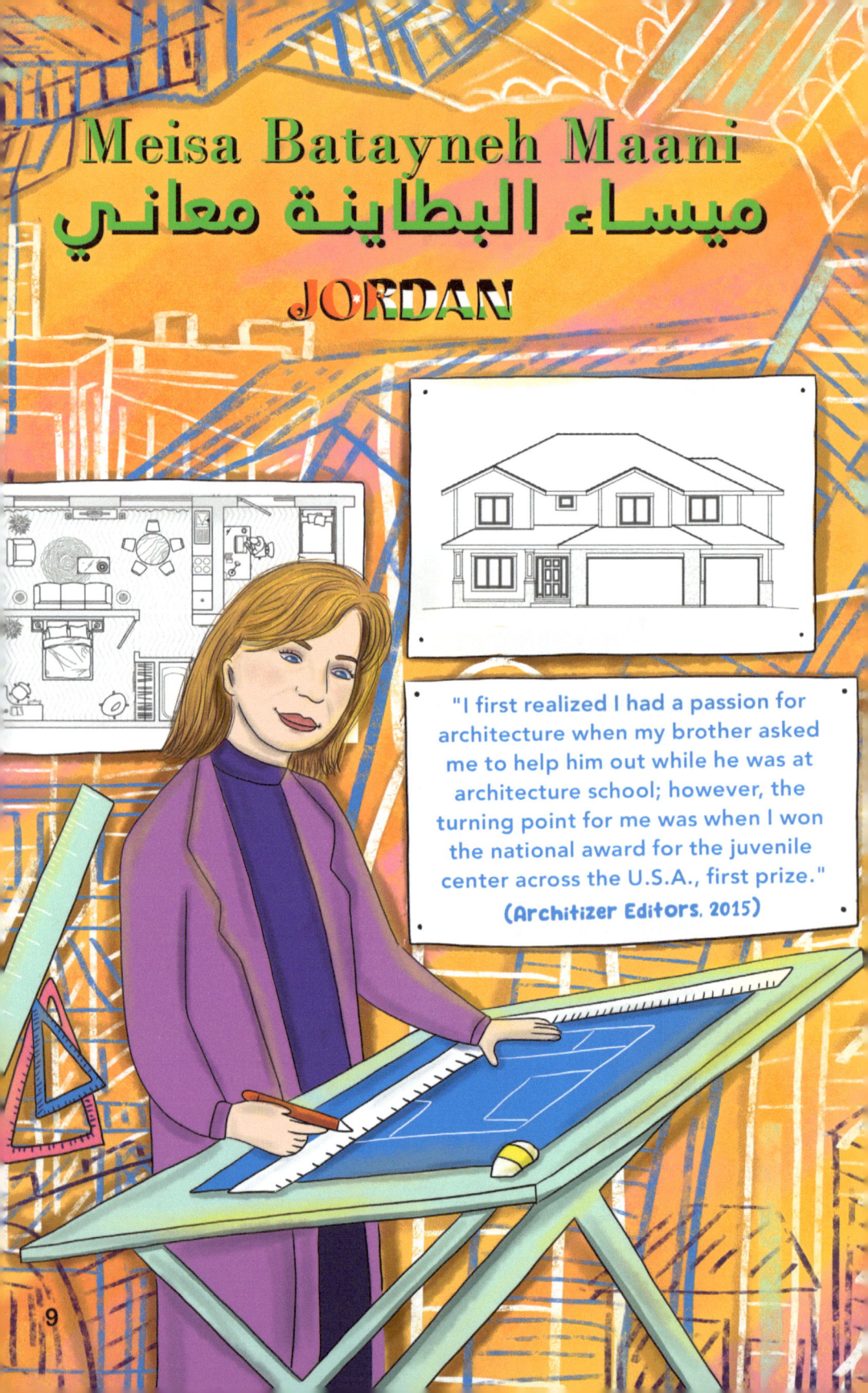

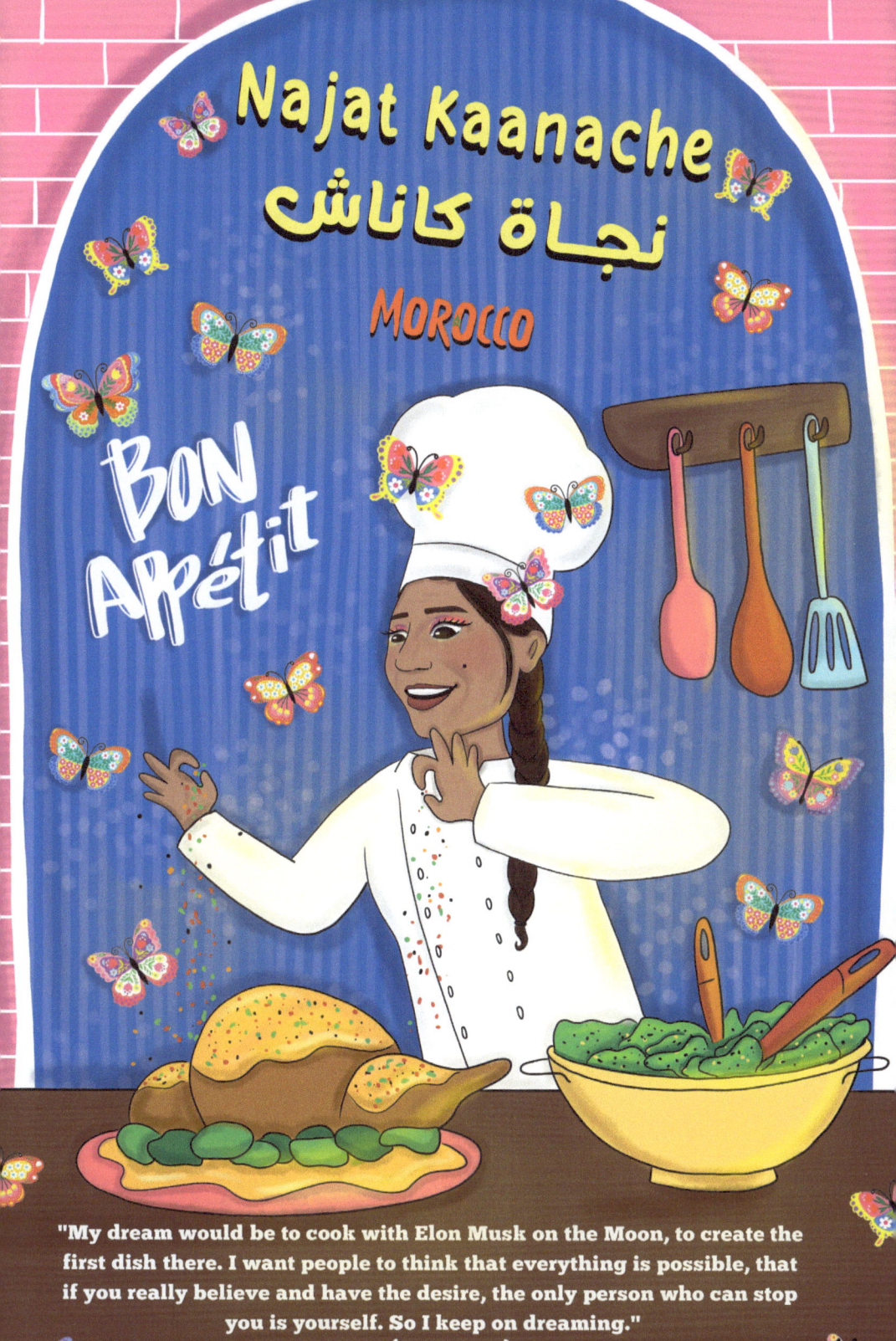

Muatasam Aulaqi

معتصم العلاقي

OMAN

"We're trying to take the company to a global level. We think wellness and cultural immersion trips will be very scalable for us."

(Coletti, 2022)

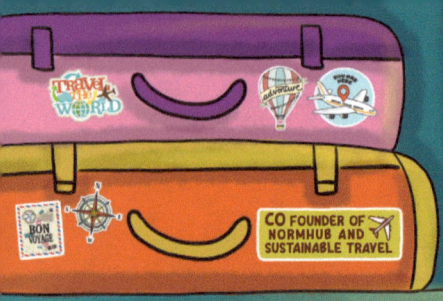

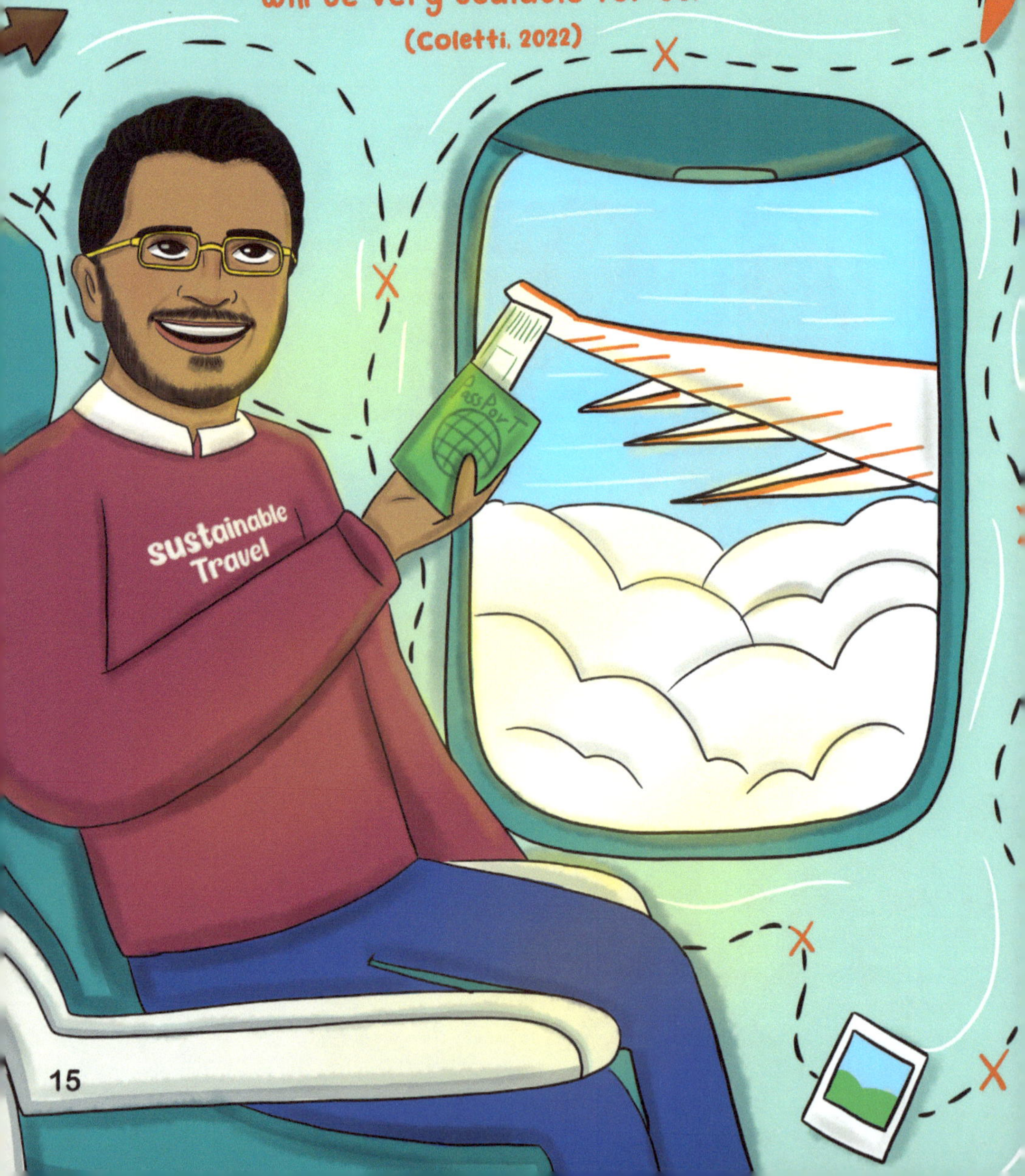

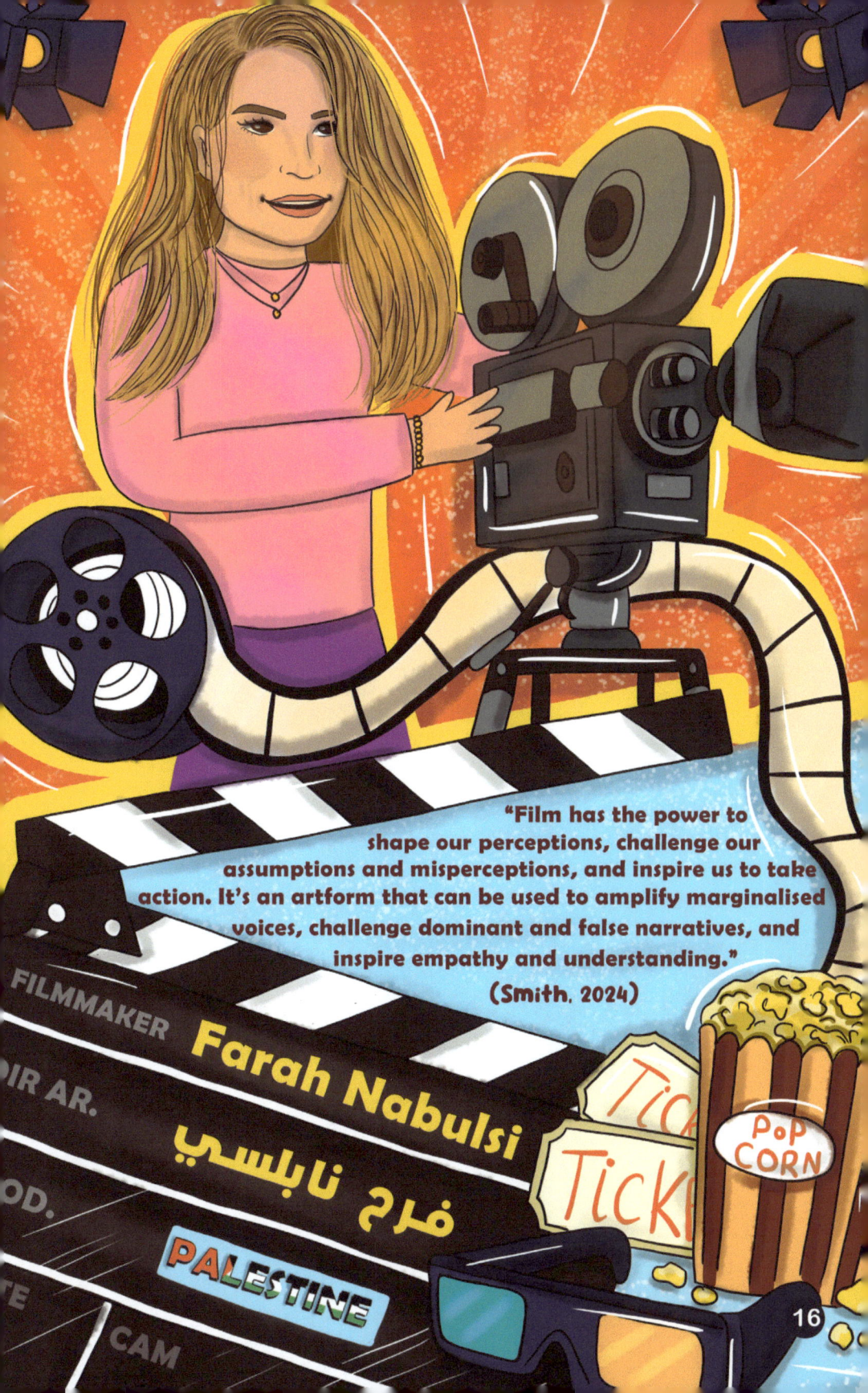

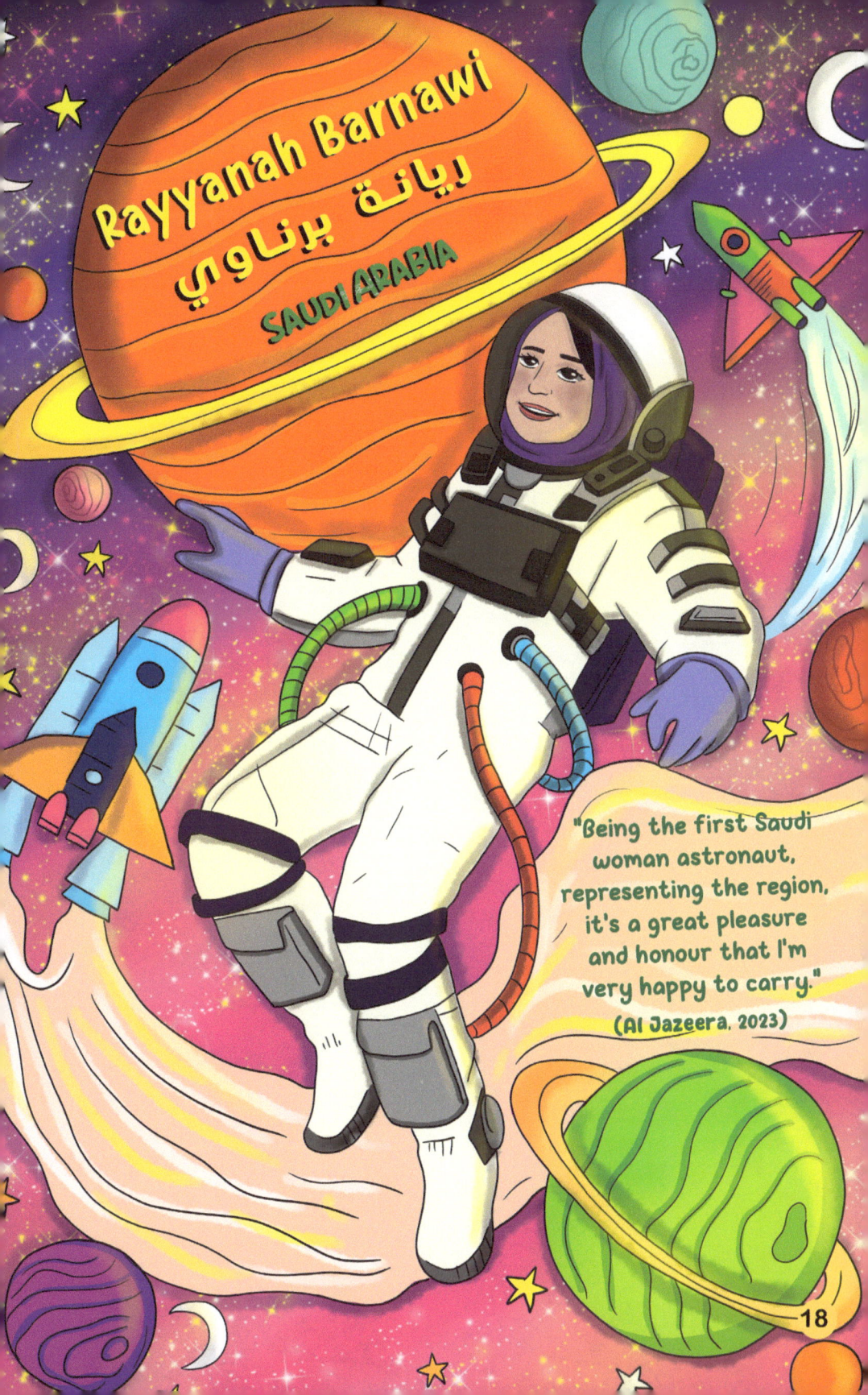

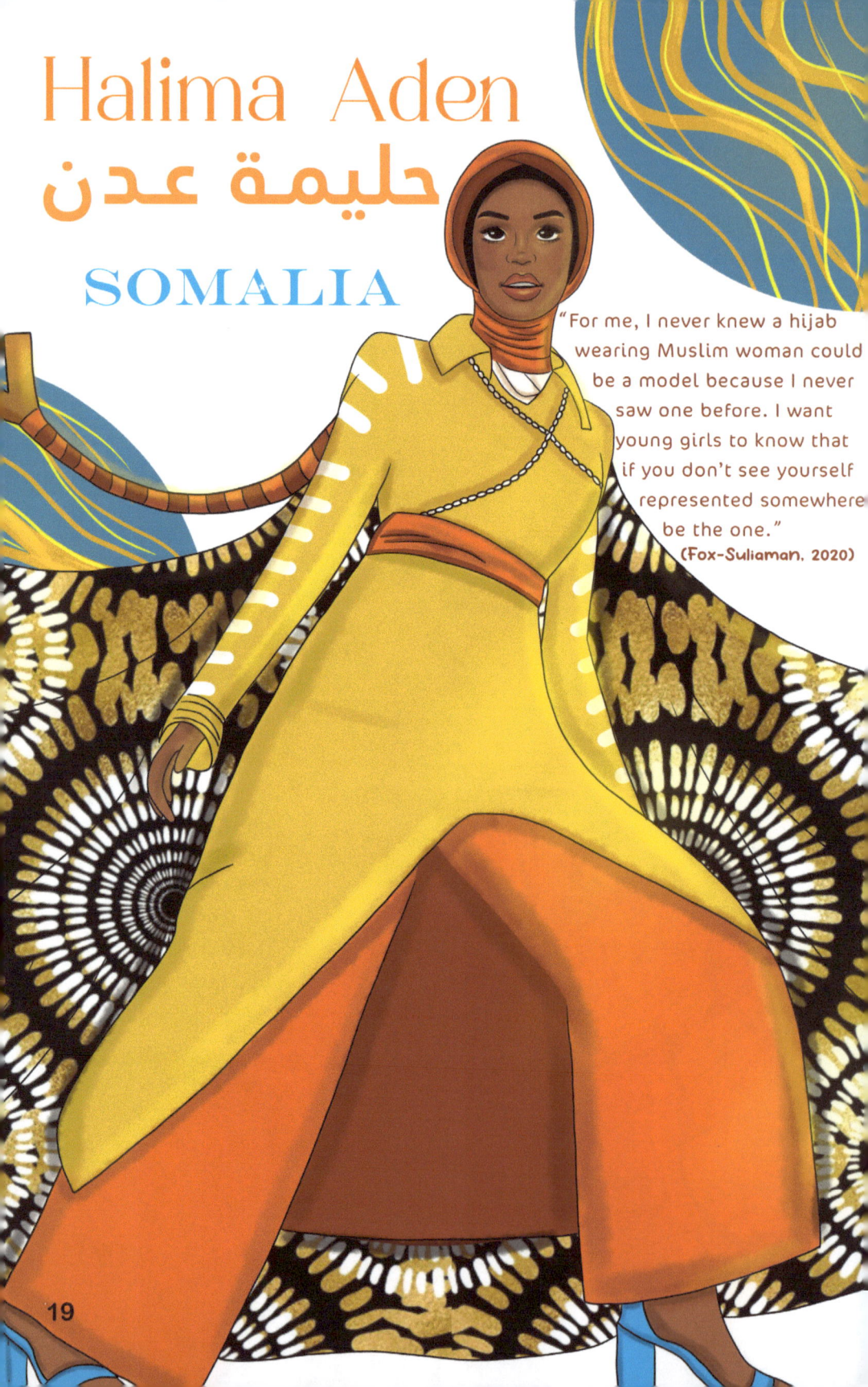

Nader Masmoudi
نادر مسعودي
TUNISIA

"I urge young people to get inspiration and guidance from the sources of learning, acquire mastery in science, and attach real importance to scientific research for the purpose of achieving scientific advancement and civil progress."

(Masmoudi, 2022)

ZAHRA LARI
زهرة لاري
UNITED ARAB EMIRATES

"All athletes have some challenges, that's normal. For me, the main thing is to keep pushing myself, ignore the negativity and just focus on my goals."
(The Design Museum, n.d.)

These amazing people show us that we can dream big and make a difference.

Just like them, we can do great things if we work hard and believe in ourselves!

What's your big dream?

Cheb Khaled
Singer and Musician

Maryam Maher
Gamer

Youssouf M'Changama
Footballer

Abdourahman Waberi
novelist, essayist, and poet

Rami Malek
Actor

Najla Imad
Paralympic Table Tennis Player

Meisa Batayneh Maani
Architect

Bazza Alzouman
Fashion Designer

Shereene Idriss
Dermatologist

Noor Tagouri
Journalist

Biram Dah Abeid
Human Rights Activist

Works cited

"Afropop Interview with Khaled." *AfricaFocus*, 2007, www.africafocus.org/docs02/pop0202.php. Accessed 15 Dec. 2024.

Alexander, Ella. "Noor Tagouri Is Revolutionizing How the Muslim Community Is Seen." *Harper's Bazaar*, 8 Mar. 2022, www.harpersbazaar.com/uk/culture/culture-news/a39299770/noor-tagouri-interview/. Accessed 15 Dec. 2024.

AAl-Smith, Gary. "Ghana Group Watch: Comoros Captain Youssouf M'Changama Says 'We Are Not a Team Who Thinks About Pressure, No, We Try to Prepare the Game Well and After All We Will Make the Best Performance as Possible and God Will Decide.'" *Facebook*, 7 June 2024, www.facebook.com/gary.africa/videos/-ghana-group-watchcomoros-captain-youssouf-mchangama-says-there-is-no-pressure-d/1308655713856050/. Accessed 15 Dec. 2024.

"Amna is a Sudane"Amna Is a Sudanese Painter—Her Work Mixes Mediums, but Her Messages About Women's Empowerment Stay Steady Throughout." *Artist Interview*, interview by Art Direction Shows, artdirection.show/interviews/amna-elhassan. Accessed 15 Dec. 2024.

"Amna Khaled Al-Obaidli: First Qatari Female Pilot Says It Wasn't Easy." *News Trail*, www.newstrailqatar.com/amna-khaled-al-obaidlifirst-qatarwww.newstrailqatar.com/amna-khaled-al-obaidlifirst-qatari-female-pilot-says-it-wasnt-easy/. Accessed 15 Dec. 2024.

Arora, Naman. "It's Game On!" *Gulf Weekly*, 3–9 June 2020, www.gulfweekly.com/Articles/41883//It%E2%80%99s-game-on. Accessed 15 Dec. 2024.

Assomull, Sujata. "Meet Bazza Alzouman, Who Designs Red-Carpet Fashion for Real Women." *Arab News*, 6 Aug. 2019, www.arabnews.com/node/1536406/lifestyle. Accessed 15 Dec. 2024.

"Athlete and Face of Nike Pro Hijab Q&A with Zahra Lari." *The Design Museum*, www.designmuseum.org/exhibitions/beazley-designs-of-the-year/fashion-20xx/nike-pro-hijab/qa-with-zahra-lari. Accessed 15 Dec. 2024.

Bakht, Syed Shayaan. "7-Year-Old Syrian Girl Sham Al-Bakour Wins Arab Reading Challenge." *Gulf Today*, 10 Nov. 2022, www.gulftoday.ae/News/2022/11/10/7-year-old-Syrian-girl-Sham-Al-Bakour-wins-Arab-Reading-Challenge. Accessed 15 Dec. 2024.

Coletti, Claudine. "Exclusive: Muatasam Aulaqi, Cofounder of NomuHub, Is Making Sustainable Tourism Mainstream for Middle East Travelers." *Forbes Middle East*, 8 Oct. 2022, www.forbesmiddleeast.com/innovation/under-30/muatasam-aulaqi. Accessed 15 Dec. 2024.

Doucleff, Michaeleen. "She May Be the Most Unstoppable Scientist in the World." *NPR News*, 20 June 2017, www.npr.org/sections/goatsandsoda/2017/06/20/530803655/she-may-be-the-most-unstoppable-scientist-in-the-world. Accessed 15 Dec. 2024.

Citations show where you found your information so others can check it too!

"Faces of Entrepreneurship: Dr. Shereene Idriss, PillowtalkDerm." *Nasdaq Entrepreneurial Center*, 9 Feb. 2023, www.nasdaqcenter.org/2023/02/09/foe-shereen-idriss-pillowtalkderm/. Accessed 15 Dec. 2024.

"First Saudi Astronauts to Blast Off in Private Mission to ISS." *Al Jazeera*, 21 May 2023, www.aljazeera.com/news/2023/5/21/first-saudi-astronauts-to-blast-off-in-private-mission-to-iss. Accessed 15 Dec. 2024.

Fox-SuliFox-Suliaman, Jasmine. "Talking Style, Representation, and Refugees on Screen with Halima Aden." *Who What Wear*, 26 Mar. 2020, www.whowhatwear.com/halima-aden-interview. Accessed 15 Dec. 2024.

Gross, Rebecca. "Literature's Invisible Art." *National Endowment for the Arts*, 2014, www.arts.gov/stories/magazine/2014/1/opening-world-international-look-art/literatures-invisible-art. Accessed 15 Dec. 2024.

"Iraqi Table Tennis Star Eyes Paris Gold Despite Losing 3 Limbs." *Daily Sabah*, 16 May 2024, www.dailysabah.com/sports/tennis/iraqi-table-tennis-star-eyes-paris-gold-despite-losing-3-limbs. Accessed 15 Dec. 2024.

"Maur"Mauritanian Activist Biram Dah Abeid: 'When I Was Ten, I Promised My Father That I Would Fight Slavery." *KU Leuven News*, 31 Jan. 2019, nieuws.kuleuven.be/en/content/2019/patronsaintsday-biram-dah-abeid. Accessed 15 Dec. 2024.

"Professor Nader Masmoudi: King Faisal Prize in Science 2022 Laureate." *King Faisal Foundation*, 2022, www.kingfaisalprize.org/professor-nader-masmoudi/. Accessed 15 Dec. 2024.

"Q+A: Meisa Batayneh on Designing a Contemporary Gateway to Petra." *Architizer*, 2015, architizer.com/blog/inspiration/industry/a-plus-winner-qa-maisam/. Accessed 15 Dec. 2024.

SgarSgarbi, Giulia. "Meet Najat Kaanache, the Moroccan Chef Who Dreams of Cooking on the Moon." *50 Best Stories*, 31 July 2020, www.theworlds50best.com/stories/News/najat-kaanache-nur-moroccan-chef-cooking-on-the-moon.html. Accessed 15 Dec. 2024.

Smith, Eve. "A Q&A Session with Director Farah Nabulsi About Her Film The Teacher." *The University Times*, 28 Sept. 2024, www.universitytimes.ie/2024/09/a-qa-session-with-director-farah-nabulsi-about-her-film-the-teacher/. Accessed 15 Dec. 2024.

SuSullivan, Kevin P. "Mr. Robot's Rami Malek Talks Crazy Twists and Befriending Christian Slater: Interview." *Entertainment Weekly*, 5 Aug. 2015, ew.com/article/2015/08/05/mr-robot-rami-malek-interview/. Accessed 15 Dec. 2024.